Security Leader Insights
for Business Continuity

Security Leader Insights for Business Continuity

Lessons and Strategies from Leading Security Professionals

Phil Hopkins, Contributing Editor

AMSTERDAM • BOSTON • HEIDELBERG • LONDON
NEW YORK • OXFORD • PARIS • SAN DIEGO
SAN FRANCISCO • SINGAPORE • SYDNEY • TOKYO

Elsevier
Radarweg 29, PO Box 211, 1000 AE Amsterdam, Netherlands
The Boulevard, Langford Lane, Kidlington, Oxford OX5 1GB, UK
225 Wyman Street, Waltham, MA 02451, USA

ISBN: 978-0-12-800839-3

Library of Congress Cataloging-in-Publication Data
A catalog record for this book is available from the Library of Congress

British Library Cataloguing in Publication Data
A catalogue record for this book is available from the British Library

For more publications in the Elsevier Risk Management and Security Collection, visit our website at store.elsevier.com/SecurityExecutiveCouncil.

ELSEVIER   Book Aid International

Working together
to grow libraries in
developing countries

www.elsevier.com • www.bookaid.org

CONTENTS

Three experienced security professionals discuss how to deal with the unanticipated consequences of "Black Swan" events.

With insight from Francis D'Addario, former vice president of Partner and Asset Protection at Starbucks Coffee; Brad Brekke, vice president of Assets Protection for Target Corporation; and Rad Jones, instructor in the School of Criminal Justice at Michigan State University and leader of the MSU/Security Executive Council Business Continuity Alliance.

Increase your company's ability to bounce back from interruptions with these tips for developing a business resiliency program.

By Rob Rolfsen, director of global risk management for Cisco Systems; and Gino Zucca, senior manager of enterprise risk management for Cisco Systems.

A global security leader shares his experiences and strategies during the events of the Egyptian Revolution of 2011.

An interview with Jim Hutton, director of global security for Procter & Gamble.

An experienced security professional shares insight into managing emotions during the response to a crisis event.

By Dean Correia, CPP former director, corporate security, Walmart, Canada, and emeritus faculty, Security Executive Council.

of the Security Executive Council and former vice president of Partner and Asset Protection for Starbucks Coffee; and Chuck Eudy, principal at Chuck Eudy Corporate Communications Inc.

Three experts discuss the benefits of business continuity certification under the Voluntary Private Sector Preparedness Certification Program and how to prepare for certification.

With insight from Don Hubbard, former CSO, PricewaterhouseCoopers LLP; Phil Samson, principal, PricewaterhouseCoopers LLP Business Continuity Management Services; and Bill Raisch, director, International Center for Enterprise Preparedness (InterCEP), New York University.

Improve your business's preparedness and resiliency with these strategies for all-hazards risk mitigation.

By Francis D'Addario, emeritus faculty member of the Security Executive Council and former vice president of Partner and Asset Protection for Starbucks Coffee.

An experienced security practitioner shows how current crisis response and business continuity practices have been shaped by past catastrophic events.

By Francis D'Addario, emeritus faculty member of the Security Executive Council and former vice president of Partner and Asset Protection for Starbucks Coffee.

INTRODUCTION

Current business continuity practices are heavily influenced by catastrophic events of recent memory—think the terrorist attacks on September 11, 2001, the 2004 Indian Ocean earthquake and tsunami, Hurricanes Katrina (2005) and Sandy (2012). In the aftermath of these events and others, it became all the more apparent that not preparing your business for the worst was a costly—and sometimes irreversible—mistake.

The threats to businesses, of course, don't begin and end with terrorism and natural disaster. To find out what really keeps business continuity professionals up at night, in late 2012 the Business Continuity Institute conducted a survey in which respondents were asked to rank 29 threats by level of concern.[1] The top six threats were identified as:

1. Unplanned IT and telecom outages
2. Data breach
3. Cyber attack
4. Interruption to utility supply
5. Adverse weather
6. Security incident

These threats and others cannot always be predicted. However, it is possible to prepare for their impact and mitigate their consequences. There are many good reasons to develop a business continuity or preparedness program, and *Ready*, a national public service advertising campaign of the Federal Emergency Management Agency (FEMA), provides a compelling list of goals that can be achieved with such a program:

- Protect the safety of employees, visitors, contractors, and others at risk from hazards at the facility. Plan for persons with disabilities and functional needs.
- Maintain customer service by minimizing interruptions or disruptions of business operations.
- Protect facilities, physical assets, and electronic information.

[1]Business Continuity Institute, *Horizon Scan 2013 Survey Report*, accessed July 1, 2014, http://www.bcifiles.com/BCI_HorizonScan2013.pdf.

- Prevent environmental contamination.
- Protect the organization's brand, image, and reputation.[2]

As security professionals, what can we do to ensure all our employees are protected from the threats mentioned above? How can we protect the reputation of the company's brand? There is no easy answer to either of these two questions. However, we can look to the experiences of our peers to find shared strategies and possible solutions for the management of our information.

In *Security Leader Insights for Business Continuity*, we have tapped some of the industry's most distinguished security professionals for their opinions and expertise.[3] This collection of timeless best practices is a quick and effective way to bring staff and/or contractors up to speed on topics related to crisis management, business resiliency, public-private partnerships, brand protection, and more. The short, straight-to-the-point chapters provide the reader with an easily accessible overview of current issues in information protection.

In the event you are forced to make rapid, significant change within your business or organization, this resource can help guide transformational change. Instead of re-inventing the wheel when faced with a new challenge, these proven practices and principles will allow you to execute with confidence, knowing that your peers have done so with success.

Phil Hopkins
Vice president of global security,
Western Union Financial Services

---

[2]"Program Management," *Ready*, accessed July 1, 2014, http://www.ready.gov/program-management.
[3]Please note that the security practitioners who contributed to these articles may no longer be at the companies listed at the time this book is published.

CHAPTER 1

When the Unpredictable Occurs

With insight from Francis D'Addario, former vice president of Partner and Asset Protection at Starbucks Coffee; Brad Brekke, vice president of Assets Protection for Target Corporation; and Rad Jones, instructor in the School of Criminal Justice at Michigan State University and leader of the MSU/Security Executive Council Business Continuity Alliance

It is seven years since the publication of Nassim Nicholas Taleb's book *The Black Swan*. In the book, Taleb introduces the concept of Black Swan events, which he characterizes as events that are 1) rare; 2) extremely impactful; and 3) often endowed by people—after the fact—with elements of predictability. Taleb argues that uncertainty cannot be tamed, and that it is foolish to attempt to tame it.

Historically, there has been a perception that security leaders are less than comfortable with unpredictability. If that's the case, it's understandable. After all, for many of these individuals, part of the job is knowing the future—preparing for every contingency and knowing when and how each event is likely to happen. They're also often penalized by management for not predicting or preparing for everything. But today, Taleb's Black Swan concept is integrating itself into more organizations' understanding of security, and it's proving a sensible and beneficial way to view and manage risk.

"Are we prepared? Not always. Innovative capabilities are required even when you are planful," said Francis D'Addario, former VP of Partner and Asset Protection at Starbucks Coffee, as he introduced a session of the Security Executive Council's Next Generation Security Leader development program. The session was focused on improving all-hazards preparedness and building public-private partnerships, so it's interesting how often presenters encouraged participants to accept and embrace the fact that no organization can plan for every possibility.

Yet as Taleb argues, this acceptance is surprisingly crucial to preparedness.

Brad Brekke, Vice President of Assets Protection for Target Corporation, shared some of his organization's methods for preparing for the unpredictable. "You can't plan for everything. Instead, we plan for consequences. What happens if you lose communication, transportation, energy?" he said. Planning for consequences, as Brekke puts it, is one way of broadening the organization's ability to respond to unlikely events.

Target has achieved resilience success from this planning model, and Brekke shared one example. On April 27, 2011, tornadoes in four southern U.S. states claimed the lives of 344 people and resulted in billions of dollars of property damage. Alabama was declared a federal disaster area. "We had 20 team members who lost homes and one killed," he said. "We lost power and the ability to run eight stores immediately, and we lost our distribution center in that area."

The company's first priority was accounting for the safety of all employees, and they activated plans to accomplish that through call centers, radio and newspaper ads, and local contacts. Meanwhile, generator power quickly got the local stores back online, but they couldn't be supplied because the distribution center was off the state's power grid. Target had planned carefully for the known risk of tornado damage, but, said Brekke, "we never anticipated having stores open and the distribution center closed at same moment."

Because of the company's resilience planning efforts, the fact that they hadn't specifically planned for this eventuality did not stop them from dealing with it quickly. The local teams were able to order five generators to be shipped overnight and the full distribution center ran off generator power only until local power was restored.

The fully stocked Target stores provided food and water to a community that desperately needed them as well as relief to public agencies. And, said Brekke, "Because our employees were safe and there was a plan, they were able to go into the community to volunteer to help the recovery efforts."

Another critical element of preparedness for unpredictability is partnership. Target's resilience efforts hinged on a multitude of partnerships with public agencies in the local area that the organizations had built and fostered long before the crisis arose. As Rad Jones, instructor in the School of Criminal Justice at Michigan State University and leader of the MSU/Security Executive Council Business Continuity Alliance, commented, "When your facility is on fire it's not the time to figure out who should do what." This is true both literally and figuratively.

If a Black Swan event occurs, both public agencies and private companies will be better able to handle consequences and continue operations if strong partnerships are already in place. The health of the community and the corporation are intertwined, and resilience improves when they know and can mutually leverage one another's strengths and resources. Partnerships like this are built on a foundation of communication and trust, said Jones. "It's difficult to accomplish collaboration without discussion about the interests and concerns of all the stakeholders," he continued. If that foundation is laid in advance, mitigation of incidents can occur without delay because, even if specific plans don't account for the event, the communication channels are there and multiple teams can easily work together to determine the best course of action based on plans that have been practiced.

Even organizations that invest heavily in intelligence gathering and analysis cannot predict every event that may impact their business. Consider planning for consequences and building public-private partnerships to help reinforce your resilience efforts when—not if—the unpredictable occurs.

CHAPTER 2

Building a Resilient Business

By Rob Rolfsen, director of global risk management for Cisco Systems; and Gino Zucca, senior manager of enterprise risk management for Cisco Systems

Corporations today are subject to a variety of crises that cause more damage more quickly than ever before. Bigger storms, broader scandals, larger data thefts, and more credible terrorist threats across the globe have the capacity to take down an unprepared business in a short time. Despite this, many corporations lack a comprehensive program to ensure the resiliency of their businesses in the face of a catastrophic event. Not only does this put them at greater risk in the event of a crisis, but also it deprives them of the added value of a complete business resiliency program.

Business resiliency is a relatively new term that represents an enterprise-wide state of readiness—an ability to quickly identify, react to, and recover from business interruptions of any kind. It incorporates under its umbrella the more familiar functions of emergency response, business continuity, crisis management, disaster recovery, and, to some extent, risk management.

Even when they're managed separately, these functions should be intuitively interdependent. But by unifying them under a resiliency program, a corporation can maximize the use of available resources, create a greater awareness of risk and continuity issues, and ensure that each involved group understands its responsibilities and those of its counterparts.

THE COMPONENTS OF RESILIENCY

Confusion among familiar terms like *emergency response, business continuity,* and *crisis management* often makes it difficult for executives to understand what programs they actually have in place. Before exploring how a resiliency program can tighten the bonds among its component functions, it's important to nail down some definitions.

Emergency Response

Emergency response provides the initial, on-site assessment of an incident. What is the situation, how are we impacted, and does this incident warrant further mitigative or responsive action on the part of the business? This function includes triage, e.g., emergency medical teams and first response.

Crisis Management

Crisis management is the process by which a business deals with an event that has been deemed significant. A situation has developed; now, how do we react? Crisis management teams (CMTs) respond based on a predetermined plan of action that is appropriate to the event. They communicate with other business units to assess and reassess impacted areas of the business and determine appropriate responses. This function includes everything from public relations management to evacuation and physical infrastructure analysis.

Business Continuity

Business continuity is the ability of the business to continue operations during and after a crisis situation. This generally involves preparing and implementing manual workarounds to enable the business to respond to an interruption. Business continuity often focuses on IT responsibilities, such as data backups and off-site storage. Many organizations call this function "disaster recovery."

Enterprise Risk Management (ERM)

Enterprise risk management is the discipline of holistically approaching risk across all business units and locations in the enterprise. Security risks are not the only risks considered under an ERM model. In ERM, risks include everything from currency fluctuation to geopolitical risks, business model concerns, and basic security risks. The goal is to help the business make educated decisions on how to manage risk, both to better protect the enterprise and to identify opportunities for growth and profit.

PIECING IT TOGETHER

A business resiliency program sets up a framework for all these elements of incident response that is developed and enforced at the corporate level. The result is a graduated, orchestrated incident response whose components share the goal of protecting employees and customers while maximizing shareholder value.

Escalation is built into the business resiliency model. As shown in Figure 2.1, the first group to be contacted in the event of an incident is the local emergency response team. The ERT assesses the situation and determines, based on criteria set by the business resiliency plan, whether the incident warrants alert or activation of the next level of response: crisis management. If it does, a local or regional crisis management team is called in to administer the launch of the crisis management program. All departments, including human resources (HR), travel, facilities, information technology (IT), public relations, and sales, may be represented on this team.

If regional crisis management determines that the incident will affect the corporation as a whole—again judging the incident against pre-set criteria—it will alert the next level, which is corporate crisis management. Business continuity exercises often begin at this level. The corporate CMT deals with issues such as maintaining the corporate image,

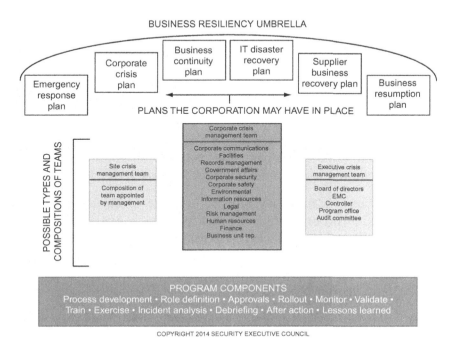

Figure 2.1 The corporate contingency planning umbrella. Copyright 2014 The Security Executive Council. All rights reserved.

aggregating information from the local CMTs, and communicating updates to individual locations and departments. Technology plays a crucial role here. A technologically advanced emergency operations center can greatly assist the corporate and regional CMTs in communicating with one another and with customers and employees, and it can also help the business track the impact of the incident across locations.

All corporate entities are held accountable for business resiliency, and crisis management and business continuity are built into every department's operational plans.

Enterprise risk management is a partner to business resiliency instead of a component of it, but its role is important to understand. Business resiliency, like ERM, deals with more than security—it aims to pull the business through any interruption, whether physical, economic, or otherwise. Only with an enterprise risk program in place can the company ensure that the business resiliency plan considers all the security and non-security risks that might impact the business.

WHAT IS THE VALUE?

Given all the crises we've seen in the United States over the past 15 years, it's surprising to discover that some organizations might not see the value in a business resiliency program. The Council on Competitiveness, a group of corporate chief executive officers (CEOs), university presidents, and labor leaders committed to enhanced U.S. competition in the global economy, has released a number of reports that show that, while the payoff of a resiliency program is sometimes difficult to quantify, it is definitely there. (See Box 2.1.)

Effective business resiliency reduces loss due to business interruption because the corporation has a practiced plan to work through and recover from the crisis as quickly as possible. The technology used for emergency operations and situational awareness may, where appropriate, find additional uses within the corporation, allowing it to become a profit center instead of a static cost.

Many companies are beginning to recognize that when they showcase their ability to bounce back from interruptions, they are strengthening their brand image and value, creating a competitive advantage.

Box 2.1 The Upside of Security

Debra van Opstal

When many CEOs hear the word *security,* they tend to think sunk cost, not strategic opportunity. For these companies, security tends to be reactive, decentralized, and ad hoc. The Council for Competitiveness has conducted studies on this topic across five industries—chemical, electric power and natural gas, financial services, oil, and pharmaceutical. Two trends emerged during our research.

First, in all of the sectors, the risk landscape is changing—and not for the better. The globalization of business in a world of technological complexity and interdependencies has vastly complicated the risk management picture. This increase in risk has also created opportunities for security that go beyond just loss avoidance.

Second, the leader companies are transforming the way they think about—and manage—security and risk. Security is "baked into" every process and investment decision, not relegated to a back-office function that is bolted onto the business.

Integrating security into business processes yields some immediate bottom-line benefits: insight into workflow efficiencies, reduced losses from fraud or waste, and savings on insurance premiums.

At Georgetown University, for example, investments in housing infrastructure—the critical component of the tuition revenue stream—led to reductions in insurance premiums. The savings were used to buy business interruption insurance, which resulted in a high bond rating and a lower cost of capital.

Some companies, such as Waste Management, are taking advantage of the technologies and capabilities developed for security to create whole new business lines. Waste Management has created a new centralized security center that not only streamlined costs across 2,000 sites but has become one of the fastest growing profit centers for the company.

For some companies, the added confidence for the brand, shareholders, customers, and employees has become an integral part of the benefits calculation. What CEOs and boards should know is that companies make money by taking risks, but they lose money by failing to manage them effectively.

Debra van Opstal is senior vice president for programs and policy at the Council on Competitiveness, a group of corporate CEOs, university presidents, and labor leaders committed to the future prosperity of all Americans and enhanced U.S. competition in the global economy.

CHAPTER 3

Leading in Crisis

An interview with Jim Hutton, director of global security for Procter & Gamble

In January 2011, the beginning of the Egyptian Revolution, local and multi-national organizations were faced with complex decisions on how to handle operations and security under the potential of escalating violence and political change. Consumer products giant Procter & Gamble closed its two plants outside Cairo and one general office in the city on January 26. (All three facilities reopened in February.) The Security Executive Council interviewed Jim Hutton, director of global security for Procter & Gamble, to talk about the experience.

SEC:	Clearly you monitor the political situation in any country where you have a facility. What methods do you use in normal times to accomplish that?
Hutton:	One of our key focus areas is to improve our external awareness. We need a capability to watch the world and hopefully protect against or preempt bad things coming our way. So we have built a Watch Officer Group here at headquarters that has global responsibility to track political, military, terrorism and crime trends. So as we see things happening, we can alert our regional resources and bring a coordinated response. I used to be a Watch Officer at the State Department, so we've tried to mimic that approach on a different scale.

SEC:	At what point did you begin to have concerns that the events in January were evolving into a major uprising?
Hutton:	One of the keys for us was our regional leader, Mark Caldwell. He was formerly with the Diplomatic Security Service, and he has worked in a number of embassies, so he's very experienced in seeing the tripwires in terms of civilian and military behavior—those signs of escalation or deterioration in the local situation. We quickly engaged with our local management team to look at a couple of indicators of problems: Is the Internet still available? What are the fuel shortages like? Things that suggest hoarding or government artificial control of certain parts of daily life in Cairo.

SEC:	Do you have hard and fast triggers for closure?
Hutton:	We do have triggers. Some of them are clearer than others. At our command center here in Cincinnati we have embedded in some software many of our key locations around the world, and we use a vendor called NC4 that tracks the situation around the key sites. If we see things like transportation or infrastructure impacts, mass movements of people, power outages— these would be some of our tripwires. A number of P&G people also have reporting responsibilities to help add context to what's going on. So it's a combination of local and international resources to help paint the picture for our decision makers.

SEC:	Once you saw the signs of a major uprising, how did that change your strategy?
Hutton:	At P&G we have a two-part crisis strategy. First, we decide which function will handle the response. If it's a crisis related to our brand or corporate reputation, our External Relations group handles that. If it's related to people and assets, that's Global Security. Once that decision is made, we employ a crisis management framework that uses a technique called PACE. This is basically about decision rights, and it can help things move quickly and stay aligned as we address the myriad facets of a crisis. The P in PACE stands for the process owner, a single person who's responsible for managing the operational aspects of the crisis team. In P&G, that is typically the local HR leader. The A is the approver, another single person who's completely accountable. So if it's a factory, it could be the plant manager, or it could be the country or general manager if more than one site is impacted. C means contributors, or people who have a technical knowledge or expertise to guide the decision makers. These could be people from security, medical, health environment and safety, supply chain—all the subject matter experts. And the E is executors, people who take action in their area of expertise, like legal, finance, and quality assurance, who would give us real-time, high-quality subject matter inputs that would help the process owners and the approvers to manage the crisis. This is a relatively new model that P&G has developed over the past two or three years, and it's really serving us well. Obviously in Cairo, the P would clearly defer to my regional manager, even though he's in a C role. A lot of people have asked why security is not the process owner. Well, there are more aspects to crisis management than just security, and we need to respect that equity.

SEC:	What specific challenges did your regional team have to overcome?
Hutton:	Mark Caldwell, my regional manager, managed this from Dubai; he wasn't even on the ground. He has evacuated thousands of people, including those from several embassies and private-sector organizations during his career, so he was the perfect person to divide up the work within his team to help support the folks on the ground in Egypt. At some point we did have a security contractor engaged on the ground to execute on our behalf, but I think it's really interesting how Mark was able to do this remotely. You'd swear he was on the ground by the timeliness and quality of his inputs. The team did a great job. The hardest work wasn't headquarters driven; it was done in the field. All the processes and systems we spent so much time and training on really came together well.

SEC:	Do the affected facilities have a mix of Egyptian and non-Egyptian employees?
Hutton:	Yes. Typically we have some expatriates (expats) or third country nationals who might be doing development assignments, highly technical roles, or general management. And obviously we have some local Egyptian employees as well as some contractors.

SEC:	What did you do to care for your local and expat employees during the crisis?
Hutton:	We did work with an evacuation provider to get our expats out, because we saw some things early on that really concerned us regarding that population. We were also deeply concerned with taking care of our local employees. We have an automated system that broadcasts messages, so we sent constant updates. We made significant interventions to make sure people had cash. We even researched the possibility of importing halal-appropriate meals ready to eat (MREs). We wound up not having to do that. But that's the level of care for our local Egyptian family members that we wanted to undertake. So health and welfare checks were very important for us.

SEC:	How was the decision made to reopen?
Hutton:	We looked again at the local situation and asked questions like, Are those tripwires improving? Is the infrastructure in place? Are the roads passable? What's the status of the curfew? Is the transport system open as far as the ability to move workers, raw material, and finished goods? What kind of guidance are we getting from local authorities in terms of freedom of movement? What is the local crime situation? We needed to look again at those kinds of tripwires to make sure they were back in a good place.

SEC:	Have you learned anything from this experience that you can translate to future events?
Hutton:	When the government or any entity impacts the communication chain—when the Internet and phones go down—a lot of the process we rely on goes down as well. We even started using runners going door to door to stay connected with our employees. So you can't be overly reliant on technology even though it provides scale and speed. It can't be a standalone solution. And we had a number of workarounds to address that. One new tool we used successfully: Our command center launched Twitter and Facebook accounts so that if our employees did manage to get to an open connection they could send us messages to ask for assistance or simply to get reassurance that there was someone they could contact if they needed help. That's a new development in our crisis management toolkit.

CHAPTER 4

When Emotions Run High: Dealing with Stress in Crisis Management

By Dean Correia, CPP former director, corporate security, Walmart, Canada, and emeritus faculty, Security Executive Council

We often talk about business continuity in practical, pragmatic terms. But it's important to remember that when a crisis hits a company, no matter how well prepared that company is, emotions will run high.

A fire or flood at a company location, a violent incident or a weather catastrophe that hits multiple stores or facilities across a region—any of these things will cause damage, injuries, and perhaps deaths. If it's your company, the people in danger are your friends and colleagues. If the disaster extends outside your organization's walls, your family may be threatened as well.

So in business continuity planning, consider not just the practical but also the emotional factors that will impact preparation, response, and recovery. Here are just a few examples.

LAYERING RESPONSE AND MANAGEMENT TEAMS

This is both a practical and an emotional consideration. I recommend that companies of any size maintain response teams at different levels in the organization. Ideally, a company will have a local response team (LRT) that acts as your eyes and hands at the site of the emergency; an incident management team (IMT), often at the home office, that comprises subject matter experts like IT, finance, media relations, and HR who can provide support to the LRT on site; and a crisis management team (CMT) made up of the senior leadership of the organization, who make decisions regarding policy and the financial aspect of the crisis. (Note: In smaller companies, the IMT and CMT might be combined.)

This layering is important for a number of reasons. Among them:

1. If you can clearly lay out a set of specific roles and responsibilities for individuals at multiple levels during a crisis, not only will you avoid confusion and improve your response, but also you will help people to concentrate their attention on explicitly defined tasks or goals, which may make it easier for them to focus in an emotionally fraught environment.
2. Having an LRT ensures that the rest of the team don't have to get their updates from CNN; you have a trusted, inside source who can answer specific questions about the situation and the well-being of the people on-site.
3. Intuitively, the team responsible for managing the crisis will be worried about the welfare of their impacted friends and colleagues and will want to go to the emergency room to check on them. But unless they're from HR, that's probably not their job during the crisis. Well-defined and well-designated team responsibilities help people to focus on accomplishing the critical functions only they can accomplish with the assurance that there is someone else who is responsible for taking care of or checking in on the injured.

CHOOSING THE RIGHT TEAM MEMBERS

The vice president (VP) of a function may not always be the right person to sit on the incident management team. Don't assume that someone with a senior title won't have a very emotional response to a crisis that will hurt his or her judgment. The individuals on the various response teams must be able to exercise their subject matter expertise with clarity and calm under pressure. Sometimes that means choosing someone farther down the ranks who will be more comfortable performing in a crisis. A high level of comfort under stress can be gained from participating in mock exercises and roundtables. By observing participants in these exercises, you can validate the performance of team members and adjust your plans and teams if necessary.

HAVING IT ALL IN WRITING

Team and company roles, responsibilities, policies, and procedures must be clearly documented and disseminated to all involved in response and recovery. When you're in your first CMT or IMT meeting and your team is frustrated, afraid, and anxious about the events happening around them, it will be easy for them to scatter their attentions, emotionally and practically, trying to take care of everything at once. You can keep people safe and on point by regularly referring to a document that says exactly what everyone needs to be doing in the situation. Someone in that meeting must be courageous enough to point to that document and remind his or her partners to stay in their roles when they want to do otherwise.

In addition, a crisis never occurs at a convenient time. You may not have all of the incident management subject matter experts in the room during the critical first hours of the incident. Having clear roles, responsibilities, and meeting tools in writing will facilitate the effective resolution of an area where someone else has to wear the hat of that function for a short time. Also, in its truest form, this documentation will allow for the crisis management function to become sustainable as a company turns over its talent.

Security directors must be the rock in crisis. It's normal for people to need a few moments to step out of a CMT meeting because they're feeling emotional. We must respect our colleagues' emotions in a crisis, and we must stand behind a strong, defined response and recovery plan to help them manage their responsibilities and our own.

CHAPTER 5

Improving Crisis Management Through Social Responsibility

With insight from Francis D'Addario, emeritus faculty member of the Security Executive Council and former vice president of Partner and Asset Protection for Starbucks Coffee

"The tragic events of today cannot be remedied with words. Our hearts go out to the victims and their families. You may be certain that although no one can predict tragedy, we have invested heavily to prevent or mitigate its consequences."

Many an unlucky CEO has had to utter a speech similar to this in the wake of disaster. Questions whirl in the minds of shareholders, stakeholders, the public, and sometimes regulators: Could this result have been avoided? Did the company do everything it could? Can corporate leaders be trusted to invest in remedying any contributing factors and cleaning up the mess?

They won't know the answers right away, but they're already forming biases and opinions based on impressions they developed last week, last month, last year. Crisis management starts well before disaster strikes, not just in the sense that the company must have risk assessments done, response plans in place, tabletops conducted, and drills tested. If the corporation has a history of acting in a socially responsible way—caring for people and communities around their sites and those of their supply chain partners—they have a better chance of bouncing back from disaster quickly and will likely suffer less reputational damage during and after the incident.

MINIMIZE REPUTATIONAL RISK

Corporate social responsibility (CSR) programs have become a must-have in recent years. There's good business sense behind this. "The ability to mitigate risk even after catastrophic mass casualty events has fairly been proven by Drs. Knight and Pretty of Oxford Metrica," says Francis D'Addario, emeritus faculty member of the Security Executive Council and former vice president of Partner and Asset Protection for Starbucks Coffee. "They studied publically traded stock valuations for 'winning' and 'losing' companies after catastrophic manmade and natural events. Their research showed in part that when you are able to react to business-interrupting crises with the assurance that you have (consistently) prioritized people, you can preserve your understood stock market value by reacting in a way that is transparent, truthful, and caring."

It comes down to this: If the company hasn't actually been caring for employees and community members in some tangible way before the crisis, it will be much harder for stakeholders to believe they care now. If the CEO comes off looking insincere, the company loses reputational capital. But if the company has been helping local schools, investing in area infrastructure, or holding health events for the community, for instance, stakeholders are likely to assume that they did all they could to protect the community from disaster and that their response will be driven by genuine concern.

"Brand confidence and loyalty are intrinsically tied to responsibility before a crisis," explains D'Addario, who is the author of *Influencing Enterprise Risk Mitigation*, a book that deals extensively with how social responsibility impacts risk management. "Starbucks Coffee's C.A.F.E. (Coffee and Farmer Equity) practices were designed with Scientific Certification Systems to assure sustainable growth and the economic viability of the supply chain, beginning with the farmer.

"Starbucks is a very people-centric culture," D'Addario continues. "People may think Starbucks is only interested in coffee plants being sustainable, but C.A.F.E. is concerned with the sustainability of people and families, in particular small farm operations, to allow that those people have the insight for growing their highest quality coffee, which Starbucks was willing to pay the highest premium prices for in the world. At the end of the day, the guarantee or warranty for having great product, which is an automatic anticipation of your consumer, is tied up in how you're caring for your supply chain and all the people in it. Reputation, barring more formidable hazards, can literally get you up the road in many of the contested regions of the world."

He goes on to explain that Starbucks supports relevant infrastructure investment in the communities surrounding the farms in their supply chain, putting money into wells, schools, and bridges. This builds brand and company loyalty in the country and community with which the company works, he says. "The general orientation of the corporate culture to do the right thing with relevant programming to give back to the community pays dividends."

In addition, it's possible that a reputation of social responsibility can actually boost profit. In 2013, a Reputation Institute study found that "73 percent of the 55,000 consumers surveyed are willing to recommend companies perceived to be delivering on CSR," whereas "only 17 percent of consumers are willing to recommend a company perceived as poorly delivering on its CSR."[1]

IMPROVE LOCAL AND GLOBAL CONTINUITY

Socially responsible decisions before a crisis can enable better business continuity, both through the global supply chain and locally.

"If you rely on someone else to provide a service that's part of the value perception of the organization," says D'Addario, "you have to make sure they're as resilient as the mother ship or they become a single point of failure."

As corporations invest in communities and people across the supply chain, they learn first-hand about the needs of those communities and their readiness for disaster. "You know who you're doing business with, what their capabilities are, and what the contingency planning is for major lapses," he says. The company can work to bridge gaps, help suppliers better ready themselves, and develop realistic contingency plans. This help is likely to be more readily accepted because of the company's dedication to community care. Says D'Addario, "This gives your organization an opportunity to be nimble enough not to be affected in the extreme by any condition—you have a business continuity plan that is going to rebound within world-class parameters."

[1]"2013 CSR RepTrak® 100 Study," Reputation Institute, accessed June 30, 2014, http://www.reputationinstitute.com/thought-leadership/csr-reptrak-100.

Likewise, socially responsible involvement can improve business continuity on a local level. Corporate headquarters and other facilities are dependent on the communities surrounding them. If a natural disaster damages local infrastructure that hasn't been adequately hardened or if it brings harm to community members—including employees and their families, consumers, and clients—the business suffers. But if the company has become engaged with the community by developing relationships with local police to assist in investigations or share resources, investing in stronger or more hardened infrastructure, hosting blood drives, or offering up its facilities for disaster assistance, the community may be stronger through the disaster and more resilient after, which in turn strengthens the company.

In addition, says D'Addario, "When individual security is assured by a community, the feelings of safety and belonging may influence selfless loyalty and the confidence to share resources to overcome community hazards."

THE VALUE OF SINCERITY

A company's investment in social responsibility in the good times, enabled by strong security and risk management, allows the CEO to stand in front of the media and the community after a disaster and say with sincerity that the company cares about the community and is truly doing all it can to help. There is significant intangible value to that kind of sincerity.

D'Addario concludes that corporate social responsibility is an invaluable tool in business-focused risk mitigation: "It builds business or organizational mission in the best of times, it protects you through the worst of times, and it gives you the benefit of the doubt while you are galvanizing your resources to react to any situation."

CHAPTER 6

Business Leading Government

By Brit Weber, program director of the Critical Incident Protocol (CIP) Community Facilitation Program with the School of Criminal Justice at Michigan State University (MSU)

You may look at the title of this chapter and think, "When does business tell government what to do?" It does happen, and for very important reasons. It begins when security executives break down the invisible walls between them and police, fire, and emergency management officials. When that happens, great opportunities can develop. I can attest to that.

As program director of Michigan State University's Critical Incident Protocol (CIP) Community Facilitation Program since 2005, I have seen what can be achieved when the public and private sectors work together. The CIP Program has worked with businesses, government agencies, and nonprofit organizations at a city, county, and regional level to bring them together for crisis management. This federally funded program, which lost its funding in 2010, led to research, best practices, and lessons learned as it worked directly at the community level to create collaborations. Michigan State University initiated partnerships with 47 communities in 24 states, with more than 4,200 public- and private-sector executives working side by side in the CIP Program workshops.

Partnerships like these offer many benefits, particularly in times of crisis. They make businesses and communities more effective in resuming normalcy and recovering after an event. They provide opportunities for resource sharing, enhanced crisis management, and critical information sharing, leading to stronger management of crisis events and minimizing impact and loss for all involved. At their best, they can also elevate the reputation of the business for its involvement in the community and public service.

Across the nation there are security executives pushing business-government collaboration that will benefit both the private and public sectors. Many times, security directors have asked me and others in the CIP program about the best ways to approach the first responder community. From my experiences and those of others, I've learned a few basic tips that will help most aspiring collaborators.

START SMALL

Don't expect to jump right into joint exercises and shared resources. The process of building a partnership begins as security executives reach out to their public-sector peers to discuss projects and programs and to share concerns.

A while ago, a security executive for an aerospace company shared with me his experience in developing a relationship with area police, fire, health, and emergency management officials. Tom, the security director, had recently joined the corporation. He was familiar with our program and the concepts we use in building a public-private partnership. He started by calling the first responder executives. On the telephone, he introduced himself and shared with them some basic information about the corporation. Afterward, he followed up by sending a brief note and a company brochure to the officials. In a few months he invited area first responder executives to their corporate facility for a 45-minute "getting to know you" event with some food and refreshments, along with a presentation on the company's preparedness and security capabilities. As time went on, Tom and his staff received some invitations from the public sector asking if they wanted to participate in meetings on community-wide evacuation planning.

Partnerships are based on trust, and they must be allowed to grow. Start small, with one of the most important issues—basic information sharing.

COMMIT

You may find that your willingness to partner is not reciprocated after a number of attempts. There may be any number of reasons for this. The important thing is to continue reaching out.

For about three years, two people in Detroit were talking with me about bringing the CIP program to their city. We were ready, but they wanted to be sure that people were committed and that the timing was right. Different conflicts or issues always seemed to prevent the initiative's launch. After three years of attempts, we facilitated the public-private partnership program for downtown Detroit. During those three years, Michigan and Detroit faced challenging economic issues, and there is no doubt that these issues can push programs to the side.

If your efforts don't pan out at first, then the timing is not right. Try later. If that doesn't work, try again later. Commitment can make things happen, just as it did for these individuals.

BE PATIENT

I recently spoke with a shopping mall security manager about the partnership program he'd had in place for a couple of years. The mall security department had a reasonably good relationship with area police and fire officials. However, the area businesses and first responder authorities had raised the partnership past the typical level. They started doing joint training and exercising. Additionally, the area security executives were invited to participate in government strategic preparedness planning projects. The security director stressed that it was a long time before he saw results that directly benefited his department and the shopping mall. He said security executives should not expect a win-win immediately.

The challenges security executives face in developing public-private partnerships are minor annoyances when weighed against the value of having such partnerships in place. Those who lead with a clear focus can easily navigate such problems and take hold of better preparedness, stronger security, and business value.

CHAPTER 7

Business Continuity and the Data Center

By Marleah Blades, former senior editor for the Security Executive Council

You may have your own server room within your company's walls, or you may outsource an off-site data center or commit your data to the cloud. Regardless of how and where you choose to keep it, your data is still your responsibility in the eyes of your constituents, customers, and, in many cases, the U.S. government.

While the phrase *data center* doesn't appear in many federal regulations, it's hiding between the lines in several high-profile rules. Business continuity is one domain in which such hidden requirements abound.

For instance, when Sarbanes-Oxley[1] section 404 talks about the adequacy of internal controls, and when Gramm-Leach-Bliley[2] says financial institutions must "protect against any anticipated threats or hazards to the security or integrity of (customer) records," data center security and business continuity are lying right there under the surface. In laws like the Health Insurance Portability and Accountability Act (HIPAA), which requires an offsite data backup plan, disaster recovery emergency plan, and emergency mode operations plans, the connection is more obvious.

When business continuity and disaster recovery are required, the data center must be considered. After all, information is king in business; if records are compromised or lost or if system failures jeopardize your ability to serve your customers, the resulting brand and operational damage can be lasting.

Having an off-site data center could be a boon in a time of disaster because damage to the facility won't damage the off-site part of the

---

[1] For more information about the Sarbanes-Oxley Act of 2002, see https://www.sec.gov/about/laws.shtml#sox2002.

[2] The Gramm-Leach-Bliley Act is also known as the Financial Services Modernization Act of 1999. For more information, see http://www.business.ftc.gov/documents/bus53-brief-financial-privacy-requirements-gramm-leach-bliley-act.

infrastructure. But when you outsource data center operation and management, you must maintain the same vigilance as you would with your own internal server room by building security requirements into your contracts. (This can be more complicated if you engage in cloud computing, where some say the lack of maturity of the product is leading to less effective contractual terms and language than out-sourced data center services.)

Here are some continuity issues to consider, whether you outsource, maintain your data center in-house, or use the cloud.

- **Have a formal business continuity plan** that is regularly revisited, tested, and revised as necessary. This is a requirement of standards including NIST and ISO 1799.
- **Make sure formal and appropriate policies exist** for the handling of emergencies and security events.
- **Have data backup off-site** so that a disaster in one location will not result in total information loss.
- **Ensure redundancy** of systems and power.
- **Have a reporting process in place** to ensure that the appropriate individuals are informed of security and continuity status and concerns.

CHAPTER 8

Planning for Pandemics

By Rad Jones, emeritus faculty, Security Executive Council, and academic specialist, School of Criminal Justice at Michigan State University

Most of us recall the news coverage and global public concern when in 2009, the H1N1 virus (known as the swine flu) caused a worldwide pandemic. While it's difficult to accurately measure just how many people were affected and how many perished during that pandemic, some estimates have suggested that between 151,700 and 575,400 deaths occurred worldwide.[1] It's possible that a similar scenario could repeat; according to the U.S. Department of Health and Human Services, "while the H1N1 viruses have continued to circulate since the pandemic, 2014 is the first season since 2009 that H1N1 has been so predominant in the United States."[2] Would your business be prepared if a pandemic were to occur again? Could you sustain your current operations if 20 percent of your workforce were absent for two weeks or more? How about 30 percent?

As flu season approaches, businesses must prepare for that possibility. The Department of Health and Human Services says that "employers play a key role in protecting employees' health and safety."[3] Many security practitioners, however, are wondering what their role should be in this preparation. If your company hasn't yet developed a plan for dealing with a widespread pandemic or if you haven't been brought into the planning, here are some points to consider.

- If your company already has an established crisis management team consisting of key company components for critical incident planning and response, you can build on that framework to develop your contingency plans for a pandemic. Joint planning creates an

---

[1]"First Global Estimates of 2009 H1N1 Pandemic Mortality Released by CDC-Led Collaboration," Centers for Disease Control and Prevention, June 25, 2012, http://www.cdc.gov/flu/spotlights/pandemic-global-estimates.htm.

[2]"H1N1 (Originally Referred to as Swine Flu)," Department of Health and Human Services, accessed June 30, 2014, http://www.flu.gov/about_the_flu/h1n1/.

[3]"Business Planning," Department of Health and Human Services, accessed June 30, 2014, http://www.flu.gov/planning-preparedness/business/index.html.

understanding of each department's area of responsibility; reduces duplication of effort, confusion, or conflict; and addresses the ongoing situation quickly.

- If your company doesn't have an established crisis management team, pull one together now. Identify the key functions of your business, find out who is in charge of each, and get them together. Don't get hung up on titles; in a small or medium business, you may not have a director of security, a director of HR, or a head of operations. But someone is a decision maker in each of those areas, and that's the person who needs to be on the team. Discuss with these business leaders what makes the business run and how they could make up for it if any one of those crucial elements was handicapped by absenteeism. That's the start of your contingency plan.
- Any pandemic planning and response must also include input from local and state health departments and information from the Centers for Disease Control (CDC; www.cdc.gov). Local and state contacts are important, since the impact of an outbreak will vary across geographic locations.
- As in any crisis planning, security must be an integral partner with other company entities (human resources, medical, operations, legal, etc.) in planning for a possible pandemic. As a part of the planning team, security can provide advice and guidance on procedures that will have an impact on the protection of company assets (people, property, information, and reputation). Security must be involved in decisions for alternate work environments or locations for employees, work-from-home strategies, procedures for distancing at-work employees from the risk of infection, restriction or cancellation of non-essential business travel, and possible disruptions while traveling overseas. Security must have an understanding of human resources, legal, and operational concerns prior to implementing their security procedures.
- Overseas travelers should be provided with information on what to expect if they are confronted with a suspected pandemic flu situation while traveling, and plans should be in place for the care of business travelers infected while they're away. The company should make arrangements with their travel department or contract agency on procedures for conveying important pandemic flu information to traveling employees or executives.

It is important to communicate to employees what to expect if the company and community are impacted by a pandemic. There will be many issues outside the control of the business that may impact operations. For example, if schools are closed, what impact will this have on the workforce? If other businesses in the community close, will this impact the company's supplier or customer base, and will employees want to know why their company is not in sync with the community? With these external conditions influencing the business, the senior security executive should have networking in place with other corporate security executives and their counterparts in the public sector. Employees must have confidence in the information they are receiving, and this can only be accomplished with good coordination between company components and also with outside agencies. Confusion can be eliminated if company employees have an understanding of company policies and procedures prior to a pandemic.

Since security needs to maintain its staffing levels and its capability to protect company assets, consider the impact the pandemic may have on security personnel. Security personnel should be thoroughly briefed on company policies, personal protection, and how to respond to suspected cases, and they should be provided with appropriate protective gear. A good idea is to conduct a tabletop exercise on a pandemic scenario with key members of the team to discuss responding to a pandemic. This will help to improve the team's response and also to illuminate any deficiencies in the plan.

There are many resources freely available to assist security and the crisis management team in their preparations. The government website www.flu.gov contains extensive planning documents, including checklists for businesses as well as individual and family planning guides.

Guidance for businesses considering stockpiling antiviral drugs can be obtained from "Considerations for Antiviral Drug Stockpiling by Employers in Preparation for an Influenza Pandemic" (http://www.flu .gov/planning-preparedness/business/antiviral_employer.pdf). Security can also obtain information from the Overseas Security Advisory Council (OSAC) http://www.osac.gov/ or the CDC travel website www.cdc.gov/travel on overseas travel situations.

CHAPTER 9

Preventing Brand Damage from Web-Based Incidents

With insight from Rad Jones, emeritus faculty, Security Executive Council, and academic specialist, School of Criminal Justice at Michigan State University; Kathleen Kotwica, executive vice president and chief knowledge strategist, Security Executive Council; Francis D'Addario, emeritus faculty member of the Security Executive Council and former vice president of Partner and Asset Protection for Starbucks Coffee; and Chuck Eudy, principal at Chuck Eudy Corporate Communications Inc.

In this chapter, four experienced security professionals respond to the question, how might I respond to a web-based incident that causes significant brand damage?

Rad Jones, emeritus faculty, Security Executive Council, and academic specialist, School of Criminal Justice at Michigan State University

Crisis management helps to protect four types of assets: people, property, information, and reputation. When I talk to a company about crisis response, I emphasize the importance of a crisis management team that includes key executives from human resources, marketing, legal, operations, security, and other key functions. The same processes used to prepare for a fire, an explosion, or severe business disruption are also helpful in preparing for a web-based threat to the company's reputation. What is the damage to the product? What is the marketing and sales recovery strategy? What are the legal options and concerns? Are there proprietary information issues? What is the financial impact? The crisis management team process brings everyone to the table to discuss how to respond. Tabletop exercises prior to an incident will help the team respond during an event. You don't have to decide things under fire if you have already considered critical incidents in a relaxed and thoughtful atmosphere.

Kathleen Kotwica, executive vice president and chief knowledge strategist, Security Executive Council

If there is already significant brand damage, it is too late to ask the question. The most important activity surrounding brand damage incidents, whether or not in the web world, is to have a brand reputation crisis strategy. First, assess the possible risks based on your company or industry. Based on that exercise, craft a response plan to include process scenarios, roles, and responsibilities. Brand damage on the web can happen fast, so the corporate response must be equally fast and should use the same channels in which the offending information surfaced. If a company is not prepared, a quick response could backfire because it's not appropriate to the audience's concerns (e.g., corporate double-speak). The keys for this audience are transparency of corporate reaction and being able to communicate a response quickly, even if it is only an assurance the company is assessing the issue and/or that appropriate action is imminent.

Francis D'Addario, emeritus faculty member of the Security Executive Council and former vice president of Partner and Asset Protection for Starbucks Coffee

It may be more valuable to ask, "How do I influence the nimble and relevant response required to preclude or mitigate brand damage from a web-enhanced incident?" The incidents range from alleged, fictitious, or fraudulent claims to true, newsworthy events that shake consumer or investor confidence. Compliance-related threats to public safety typically broaden stakeholder concerns as government agencies enter the fray. Depending on the incident allegation, oversight can include local, state, or federal health or law enforcement agencies. Brand messaging must be relevantly directed to any engaged audience. Ensure cross-functional emergency preparedness or crisis teams (communications, operations, quality assurance, legal, security, etc.) are well advised to anticipate all-hazards risk on a pre-event basis, to draft priority messaging, to enumerate persuasive mitigations, to transparently acknowledge the gravity of the allegation, and to demonstrate conduct that stakeholders expect of a world-class brand. Always keep audiences informed of developments via web sites, social media, and other consumer and investor channels.

Chuck Eudy, principal at Chuck Eudy Corporate Communications Inc.

In today's technology-for-all world, anyone with a $30 smartphone or an entertaining opinion blog can unintentionally or deliberately destroy your sales trajectory. They can say or show things about your company or its products that are not true and that are vastly different from the image you have invested scores of years and millions of dollars to establish. Preparing for such an incident should be mission-critical for any consumer-dependent business. You should have the processes and tools in place to identify potential web-based incidents before they spread and to harness the power of web-based discussion channels to minimize or prevent damage. Know the menu of social media and related cyber-arenas available to them and you. Know and understand Facebook, Twitter, YouTube, Digg, media-based blogs, and the trailing reader commentary. And use them thoughtfully—even entertainingly, if you have to—to address the misinformation, and do it on an attitude level consistent with each channel's users.

CHAPTER 10

Exploring the Voluntary Private Sector Preparedness Certification Program

With insight from Don Hubbard, former CSO, PricewaterhouseCoopers LLP; Phil Samson, principal, PricewaterhouseCoopers LLP Business Continuity Management Services; and Bill Raisch, director, International Center for Enterprise Preparedness (InterCEP), New York University.

In this chapter, three experienced security professionals respond to two questions:

1. Should my company seek business continuity certification under the Voluntary Private Sector Preparedness Certification Program?
2. What should I be doing to prepare, and how do I show cost benefits of certification?

Should my company seek business continuity certification under the Voluntary Private Sector Preparedness Certification Program?

Don Hubbard, former CSO, PricewaterhouseCoopers LLP

In today's threat environment, it is imperative that each organization inculcate the concept of resilience into its culture so that the enterprise may not only survive but also thrive in the aftermath of an incident or disaster. I believe one of the best ways to do so is to have robust business continuity plans that show clear accountabilities and are exercised frequently. A big part of exercising plans is identifying gaps. Going through the certification process will help identify gaps and demonstrate to top management that the organization is as prepared as possible.

Phil Samson, principal, PricewaterhouseCoopers LLP Business Continuity Management Services

For companies that have invested in their business continuity management (BCM) program—including a related risk management governance organization and procedures, periodic testing and update of critical components, and ongoing evaluation of exposures—certification will help validate for management and key stakeholders the robustness of the BCM program. For those organizations that have less (or no) emphasis on BCM, now would be a good time for individuals with risk management responsibilities to use the tenets of the certification program to build an internal business case for a stronger BCM focus. Early adopters may begin applying for certification within the next year, and these early adopters may be your customers or key business partners, who will start asking when your BCM program will undergo the same certification process.

Bill Raisch, director, International Center for Enterprise Preparedness (InterCEP), New York University

A company should pursue certification only if it offers potential business value. The certification will provide (a) an accepted method to confirm that key elements of organizational resilience are in place, and (b) the opportunity to use that metric to realize business benefits. The program is currently in development and optimally will allow you to measure resilience either on your own, with a related "second party" (e.g., a customer/supplier relationship), or via unrelated "third party" certification (outside auditor). A clear metric could be used to more effectively manage enterprise-wide efforts. We have several hundred firms involved right now in working groups to advance benefits to businesses and evaluate the use of certification in assessing supply chain resilience, minimizing legal liability, and providing companies with a measure to be shown to insurance companies and rating agencies to potentially realize benefits in insurance and credit ratings and also in public reporting for both reputational and compliance advantages—all to more clearly link resilience with bottom-line benefits over time.

What should I be doing to prepare, and how do I show cost benefits of certification?

Don Hubbard

The first step, in my view, is to identify the key elements of the various standards which may be adopted into the certification program and then overlay those elements onto the organization's existing plans. Standards specifically mentioned are NFPA 1600, ISO/PAS 22399-2007, and British Standard (BS) 2599. Some gaps likely will be apparent and remedial steps can be taken. While there are currently no concrete financial incentives to go through the certification process, many believe market forces will make it a de facto requirement, much as the Payment Card Industry standards are now virtually mandated by the marketplace. In addition, many believe the plaintiff's bar, rating agencies, boards of directors, audit committees, institutional investors, stockholders, business partners (e.g., vertical supply chain), and other key stakeholders will encourage certification.

Phil Samson

The certification cost-benefit process should start with the results of your business impact analysis and BCM strategy where key external parties (e.g., customers, vendors, outsourcers, business partners) were identified. While the certification process can provide senior management with an indication that your BCM program is achieving the certification program's objectives, a significant benefit of the program is the additional comfort that your key external parties derive, knowing that you've taken steps to minimize the impact to them of a business interruption. In some form or fashion, most companies are part of a supply chain, and an interruption in any part of the supply chain can impact the entire supply network. We foresee in the near future that this certification program will be used within the vendor/business partner due diligence process, providing the companies that are certified a distinct advantage over those that aren't.

Bill Raisch

The first steps in evaluating the certification might include (1) educating yourself on the program and potentially joining a working group (info available at www.nyu.edu/intercep); (2) pursuing internal conversations with potentially interested parties in supply chain management, risk management, insurance, compliance, legal, etc.; and (3) an internal self-assessment to one or more of the standards when they are identified.

CHAPTER 11

Emergency Preparedness: Compliance, Care, and the Long View

By Francis D'Addario, emeritus faculty member of the Security Executive Council and former vice president of Partner and Asset Protection for Starbucks Coffee

Our current fluid global risk cannot be read in the carefree faces of children at play. They are blissfully unaware of foreboding hazards that endanger them and their protectors. In fact, the multi-trillion-dollar all-hazard landscape, most vividly rendered by the World Economic Forum's 2014 Global Risk Report, remains unknown to many. (The report, which outlines some of the issues most likely to come to the fore of the global risks landscape and describes their interconnectedness, can be downloaded from http://www3.weforum.org/docs/WEF_GlobalRisks_Report_2014.pdf). Those with insight into these risks have a duty to help increase others' awareness of them and to measure mitigation progress.

If we hope to lead our organizations through this complex global risk landscape, we must learn what we can from manmade and natural risk events to improve preparedness and resiliency. Effective risk mitigation requires investments of time, money, and mindshare. We must assess our current capabilities and close the gap on the people, process, and technology resources we need to ensure a more resilient future.

Clearly, even the most aware and prepared family, institution, community, and nation state is not immune to catastrophes such as accidents, crime, terror, severe weather, and tectonic events. Yet our relative individual preparedness and nimble cross-sector response to imminent threats can mitigate far more serious consequences to our emotional, physical, and fiscal health.

COMPLIANCE IS A PARTIAL SOLUTION

Those of us who are skeptical about our organizational leadership's commitment to all-hazards preparedness may be heartened by evolving liability and regulatory recommendations. The U.S. Department of

Homeland Security has developed the Voluntary Private Sector Preparedness Accreditation and Certification Program (PS-Prep).[1] Thanks to the 9/11 Commission, this program attempts to improve private-sector preparedness for disasters and emergencies. The adopted standards include those of the National Fire Protection Association, the British Standards Institution, and ASIS International.

Each standard is valuable and merits serious review. Collectively, they are helpful to those who have not yet undertaken an all-hazards risk mitigation assessment or plan. Others will find them useful for formulating gap analyses. But for those who are inclined to think that preparedness is now the law of the land, I urge caution.

While PS-Prep is a step forward, it is still a voluntary program. Because of the recent near-collapse of the global financial system, with its arguable failure of risk oversight and resulting contraction of resources, security planners and their cross-functional risk mitigation teams face an uphill struggle. Even organizations that are inclined to comply with PS-Prep or to advance preparedness in other ways may be constrained by smaller purses, downsized capacity, and skeptical program supporters who have witnessed billions of dollars in global security investment since 2001 with little persuasive return on investment. Add to those concerns the reality that these voluntary standards will compete with other government mandates, including state and federal requirements, around commercial and health care information protection including PCI data security standards and HIPAA.

Compliance alone is only a partial solution. We must help our organizational leaders find deeper motivation for improved preparedness by focusing on stakeholder confidence and shareholder value.

CULTURE OF CARE

Corporate entities, governments, and not-for-profits all depend on stakeholder confidence. Customers, citizens, donors, employees, investors, suppliers, and their dependents have increasing expectations of care. Cared-for and engaged stakeholders are more productive in core process performance. People-care can also protect brand reputation;

[1]For more information about PS-Prep, visit https://www.fema.gov/about-ps-preptm.

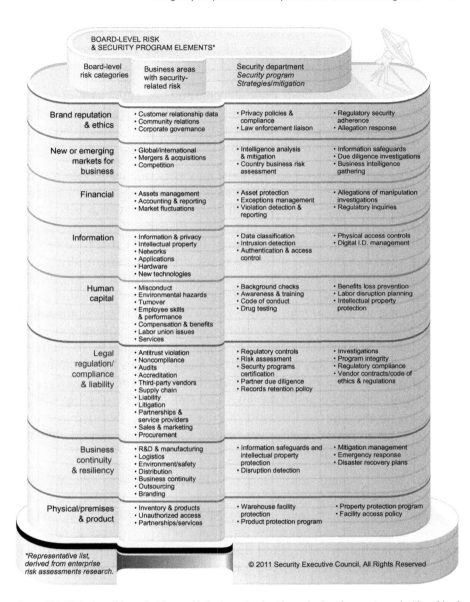

Figure 11.1 Mitigating all-hazards risk arguably begins and ends with people. Brand reputation under "board-level risk" (top left) is dependent on human capital protections (bottom left to right) that are expected of the brand. Hazard awareness, preparedness, risk detection, and response are required in a culture of care.

when an event does occur, companies that have shown a high standard of care for their people are more likely to enjoy the "benefit of the doubt" in the public mind.

Responsible leaders heed these expectations of care, as well as the increasing relevance of board-level risk, which has been shown through research and articulated by the Security Executive Council. Some of their concerns are illustrated in Figure 11.1.

More influential metrics on this issue may persuade leadership toward a path of sustainable resiliency. Ultimately "the metric" for private sector stakeholder confidence is market valuation. Company worth before and after major catastrophic events is instructive. One recent calamity, the BP oil spill in April 2010, supports the point. In the months that followed the incident, market valuation of the company dropped dramatically. *CNN Money* reported that "Fitch Ratings downgraded BP for a second time this month [June 2010] to just above junk status, as the news just keeps getting worse for the oil giant. Fitch said it lowered its senior unsecured rating to BBB from AA, in response to increasing estimates of spilled oil in the Gulf of Mexico and increasing pressure on the oil giant to establish an escrow account to pay for damages."[2] Value metrics like this must be made clear to organizational leadership. The stakes for emergency preparedness go beyond compliance fines and sanctions. Leadership will be judged on people-care. In the court of public opinion, the organizational outcomes for apparent negligence before, during, and after a disaster bode additional peril, if not doom.

Drs. Rory Knight and Deborah Pretty conducted decade-long research of 74 firms, following their involvement in aviation disasters, fires and explosions, seismic catastrophes, and terrorist attacks. While few will argue that mass casualty situations offer a worst-case risk scenario for shareholder value, their findings are also informative for other types of disasters as well. Following is a summary of their main findings:

1. *Mass casualty events have double the impact on shareholder value....*
2. *The market makes a rapid judgment on whether it expects reputation to be damaged or enhanced ... in the case of mass fatality events ... it takes ..., on average, 100 trading days to emerge prominently.*

---

[2]Aaron Smith, "Fitch Downgrades BP ... Again," *CNN Money*, June 15, 2010, http://money.cnn.com/2010/06/15/news/companies/bp_fitch_rating_downgrade/index.htm.

3. As with non-fatal reputation crises for firms ... value recovery relates to the ability of senior management to demonstrate strong leadership and to communicate at all times with honesty and transparency.
4. [T]he sensitivity and compassion with which the chief executive responds to victim's families and the logistical care and efficiency with which response teams carry out their work are paramount.
5. Irrespective of whose responsibility is the cause ... a sensitive managerial response is critical to ... shareholder value.[3]

Our relative success as asset protection professionals and risk mitigators will likely be determined by our organizational leadership performance. We have the opportunity to influence.

TAKING THE LONG VIEW

We know the long view and a diverse data set are required to calculate catastrophic impacts. Similarly longer views are required for forward-looking, cross-functional risk mitigation teams. To that end, Bob Hayes, managing director of the Security Executive Council, recently introduced an initiative called Security 2020™. He stated, "Board-level risk requirements for people, critical process, and asset protection are increasingly complex and require a new, collaborative, and performance-based approach with practitioners, manufacturers, and service providers."[4] Our aim must be to persuasively influence continuous solutions innovation with return on investment and risk mitigation improvement through the next decade.

No single entity can own emergency preparedness. Process and technology convergence guided by organizational mission will enable intradepartmental strategic plan execution with oversight by executive risk committees and the board of directors. Business continuity, communications, compliance, engineering, facilities, finance, human resources, IT, operations, procurement, risk management, and others will fund collaborative projects with return on investment (ROI) performance expectations.

[3]Rory F. Knight and Deborah J. Pretty, "Protecting Value in the Face of Mass Casualty Events," Oxford Metrica, September 29, 2005, page 4, http://oxfordmetrica.com/public/CMS/Files/601/04RepComKen.pdf.
[4]"Security Executive Council Eyes 2020 Solutions and Leadership," Security Executive Council press release, June 8, 2010, on the Security Executive Council website, https://www.securityexecutivecouncil.com/newsroom/details.html?pr=26111.

COMMUNICATIONS PROMOTE CONFIDENCE

Our ability to execute a cross-functional, operational plan with cost efficiencies, loss avoidance, and prevention earns both leadership and stakeholder confidence. Importantly, efforts that produce results will fund additional programming. Even when prevention or mitigation efforts fail, we will be given the benefit of the doubt when we have transparently communicated risk with relevant mitigation resources before an event and act responsibly thereafter. Ultimately our success will be measured by our influence for improved preparedness on the job, at home, and in the community. For cultures that care, and all their stakeholders, that is something to smile about.

CHAPTER *12*

Resilience Requires Intelligent Preparedness[1]

By Francis D'Addario, emeritus faculty member of the Security Executive Council and former vice president of Partner and Asset Protection for Starbucks Coffee

Manmade catastrophes and naturally occurring phenomena, from contagion to seismic or severe weather events, have endangered us since the dawn of civilization. Our anxiety for a range of hazards is palpable. The so-called "death of distance," a phrase coined by Frances Cairncross to describe the globe-shrinking effect of instantaneous communications, reminds us of every prevention or mitigation miss.[2]

We began this millennium with high anxiety related to the Y2K time code ambiguity. Many surmised that date-related machine processing would fail on January 1, 2000. Widespread utility grid and critical systems issues were anticipated. First responder teams were on alert throughout the world. Yet relatively little disruption occurred thanks to the mitigation efforts of program managers and their developers. It was not until 2001 that the world was shaken by multiple influencing events. On January 26, 2001, the Gujarat region of India and a portion of eastern Pakistan were devastated by an estimated 7.6+ magnitude earthquake. Estimated deaths exceeded 20,000. Injuries topped 167,000 with more than a million homes destroyed. *Pandemic Threat Posed by Avian Influenza Viruses* was also published.[3] The research finding by Taisuke Horimoto and Yoshihiro Kawaoka warned of similarities between H5N1 and the Spanish influenza H1N1 that claimed 20,000,000 victims worldwide in 1918 and 1919.

Later in 2001, on September 11, all eyes turned to the United States when primetime news footage showed the consequences of Osama Bin

---

[1]This chapter is an excerpt from *Influencing Enterprise Risk Mitigation* by Francis D'Addario (Elsevier, 2013).

[2]Frances Cairncross, *The Death of Distance: How the Communications Revolution Will Change Our Lives.* Boston: Harvard Business School Press, 1997.

[3]Taisuke Horimoto and Yoshihiro Kawaoka, "Pandemic Threat Posed by Avian Influenza Viruses," Clinical Microbiology Reviews 14, no. 1 (2001), doi: 10.1128/CMR.14.1.129-149.2001.

Laden's long-standing threat: 2,974 victims and 19 suicide terrorists died with the destruction of the twin-tower World Trade Centers of New York, and the Pentagon sustained heavy damage.

Identity theft and fraud kept pace with network expansion, enabling subjects of interest (including the 9/11 hijackers) to travel with impunity under alias credentials. Identity theft topped the U.S. Federal Trade Commission's consumer complaints in 2001. Enron, the $64 billion energy trading giant, declared bankruptcy. Failed fraud detection oversight cost the brand and all its stakeholders.

In October 2001, the Amerithrax anthrax attacks reminded the United States that domestic terrorism can be just as effectively disruptive as any imported variety. That year was also the last time the FDA visited a Blakely, Georgia, food manufacturing facility that later distributed *Salmonella*-laced product to unsuspecting consumers with fatal results. Harry Markopoulos, a certified fraud examiner, made his way for the second time to the U.S. Securities and Exchange Commission (SEC) with incontrovertible proof of the largest Ponzi scheme in history. They did not heed his warning.

LEARNING OUR WAY

The heroic recovery efforts of September 11, 2001, were well documented. The events of that year influenced crisis response and business continuity. Multiple sectors reshaped precautionary government and non-governmental organization advisories to reach diverse global audiences:

1. Evacuation and shelter-in-place guidelines
2. Procedures for mail handling and identifying or reporting suspicious packages
3. Security guidelines including facility access control and suspicion reporting
4. Travel guidelines, restrictions, and tips
5. All-channel risk reporting and status update communications protocol

The realization that all-hazards protection was required became obvious as risk-related compliance legislation was passed in every country around the world. Resulting board-level risk brought the protection portfolio into the light. Governments began to understand that arguably 90 percent of critical infrastructure is in the private-sector domain. They also learned that response to global catastrophe required all hands, including non-governmental organizations (NGOs).

THE VALUE OPPORTUNITY

The dots are there for protection professionals and others to connect. Current and evolving risk resilience requires courageous cross-functional leadership and systematic methodologies that will transcend any one group. Brand reputation in any sector will continue to be earned by those who can take a hit and bounce back. There is much work to do before, during, and after the next disasters of consequence—and there are fewer resources.

High-morbidity pandemic is still on the horizon. Networks remain both the target and the means for multinational organized crime including theft, fraud, and terror. Criminals, inside and out, continue to exploit the soft targets around the world. Critical infrastructure, including intelligence and first responder agencies, are still uncomfortably vulnerable. More than ever, supply chain and critical process management are required for both proprietary and critical dependency environments. Threat appreciation, exception detection, and response preparedness must be improved.

The failures of persuasive risk detection, compliance, and effective mitigation have left us with unnecessary injury, death, damage, loss, and deficits worldwide. Confidence has been measured at the all-time low since the Great Depression. Counterintuitively, the resultant downsizing, rightsizing and re-engineering may be a gift—if and when we re-deploy more intelligent, nimble, cross-functional, and return-on-investment—capable protection elements. Good and best practices will continue to evolve from risk intelligence linked with integrated mitigation innovation and performance.

The data is in. Brand reputation is performance dependent. Stakeholders can no longer afford only heroic efforts after the fact. They expect us to prevent and mitigate while navigating both compliance and emerging risk. Cross-functional talent, tools, and training are required to prepare for and weather the storm. Mass casualty events of the recent past inform future stakeholder expectations and valuation.

In their 2005 report, *Protecting Value in the Face of Mass Fatality Events*, Drs. Rory Knight and Deborah Pretty analyzed shareholder value impacts for a wide range of firms following mass casualty events including aviation disasters, fires and explosions, terrorist attacks, and natural catastrophes. Their research shows that the ability to manage a mass fatality event (i.e., winners) is even more impressive to investors, and the *inability* to manage such an event (i.e., losers) is even more disappointing than in less tragic corporate crises.

Our call to action demands holistic risk management. Our ability to identify effective prevention and mitigation before the fact will serve us well in all instances. Protecting people, assets, and critical process effectively protects brand and ensures community resilience.

About the Contributing Editor

Phil Hopkins is vice president of global security for Western Union Financial Services where he has responsibility for crisis management, executive protection, investigations, law enforcement relations, physical security, and travel safety.

Mr. Hopkins joined Western Union in July 2006 as vice president in the Corporate Security Department with responsibility for agent due diligence, crisis management, employee background checks, executive protection, and travel safety. In January 2011 Mr. Hopkins took over responsibility for the entire global security team.

Previously, Mr. Hopkins served as the director of corporate security for the First Data Corporation where he was responsible for executive protection and event security.

Prior to his private sector experience, Mr. Hopkins served 20 years in the United States Secret Service where he completed his career as the Assistant Special Agent in charge of the Houston Field Office. During his career he fulfilled assignments in the Charlotte Field Office, Miami Field Office, Bush Protection Division, Washington, DC, Headquarters, and the Houston Field Office.

Mr. Hopkins received a Bachelor of Science degree in Criminal Justice from Auburn University, and in 2011 he completed the Wharton School ASIS Program for Security Executives. Mr. Hopkins currently serves on the Advisory Council for the International Association of Financial Crimes Investigators (IAFCI). He is a member of ASIS International, the International Security Management Association (ISMA), the Overseas Security Advisory Council (OSAC), and the Domestic Security Advisory Council (DSAC).

About Elsevier's Security Executive Council Risk Management Portfolio

Elsevier's Security Executive Council Risk Management Portfolio is the voice of the security leader. It equips executives, practitioners, and educators with research-based, proven information and practical solutions for successful security and risk management programs. This portfolio covers topics in the areas of risk mitigation and assessment, ideation and implementation, and professional development. It brings trusted operational research, risk management advice, tactics, and tools to business professionals. Previously available only to the Security Executive Council community, this content—covering corporate security, enterprise crisis management, global IT security, and more—provides real-world solutions and "how-to" applications. This portfolio enables business and security executives, security practitioners, and educators to implement new physical and digital risk management strategies and build successful security and risk management programs.

Elsevier's Security Executive Council Risk Management Portfolio is a key part of the **Elsevier Risk Management & Security Collection**. The collection provides a complete portfolio of titles for the business executive, practitioner, and educator by bringing together the best imprints in risk management, security leadership, digital forensics, IT security, physical security, homeland security, and emergency management: Syngress, which provides cutting-edge computer and information security material, and Butterworth-Heinemann, the premier security, risk management, homeland security, and disaster-preparedness publisher. These imprints, along with the addition of Security Executive Council content, bring the work of highly regarded authors into one prestigious, complete collection.

The **Security Executive Council** (www.securityexecutivecouncil.com) is a leading problem-solving research and services organization focused on helping businesses build value while improving their ability to effectively manage and mitigate risk. Drawing on the collective knowledge of a large community of successful security practitioners, experts, and strategic alliance partners, the Council develops strategy and insight and identifies proven practices that cannot be found anywhere else. Their research, services, and tools are focused on protecting people, brand, information, physical assets, and the bottom line.

Elsevier (www.elsevier.com) is an international multimedia publishing company that provides world-class information and innovative solutions tools. It is part of **Reed Elsevier**, a world-leading provider of professional information solutions in the science, medical, risk, legal, and business sectors.

Printed in the United States
By Bookmasters